How to Attack and Defend Your Website

T0383234

How to Attack and Defend Your Website

Henry Dalziel

AMSTERDAM • BOSTON • HEIDELBERG
LONDON • NEW YORK • OXFORD • PARIS
SAN DIEGO • SAN FRANCISCO
SINGAPORE • SYDNEY • TOKYO

Syngress is an Imprint of Elsevier

Syngress is an imprint of Elsevier
225 Wyman Street, Waltham, MA 02451, USA

British Library Cataloguing-in-Publication Data
A catalogue record for this book is available from the British Library

Library of Congress Cataloging-in-Publication Data
A catalog record for this book is available from the Library of Congress

ISBN: 978-0-12-802732-5

For information on all Syngress publications
visit our website at http://store.elsevier.com/

Working together
to grow libraries in
developing countries

www.elsevier.com • www.bookaid.org

TABLE OF CONTENTS

AUTHOR BIOGRAPHY

Henry Dalziel is a serial education entrepreneur, founder of Concise Ac Ltd, online cybersecurity blogger, and e-book author. He writes for the blog "Concise-Courses.com" and has developed numerous cybersecurity continuing education courses and books. Concise Ac Ltd develops and distributes continuing education content (books and courses) for cybersecurity professionals seeking skill enhancement and career advancement. The company was recently accepted onto the UK Trade & Investment's (UKTI) Global Entrepreneur Programme (GEP).

CONTRIBUTING EDITOR BIOGRAPHY

Alejandro Caceres is the founder of Hyperion Gray, LLC, a web-security and big-data R&D company. He is also the creator of the PunkSPIDER project, an open-source web-app-vulnerability scanner and repository of vulnerabilities found on the open web. Alejandro has spoken at several major security conferences (DEF CON, ShmooCon, AppSec) and enjoys making web-app hacking principles more accessible to web developers so that they can design and build more secure applications.

INTRODUCTION

When you are trying to build a secure website or web application, it helps to see the problem through the eyes of the adversary, to understand the weaknesses that can be used to attack a website. Therefore, the goal of this book is to teach you how to hack websites. Through hands-on exercises we will show you several of the most common weaknesses and how they can be exploited by an attacker – in this case, you. After you learn this, you will be better prepared to protect your own, your clients' or your employer's websites from these types of attacks.

We will start by learning the basic web technology stack, and then we will delve a little deeper and talk about the HTTP protocol. Central to this book is being able to understand the technologies so that we can make them do exactly what we want, instead of what the developer intended, and that in itself is a good definition of "web application hacking." The next step is to learn what tools to use for web app hacking and how to set up those tools[1]. After that, the fun begins – exploitation and learning how to break web applications.

To finish up, we will talk about finding vulnerabilities in websites, which will again help you see from the adversary's perspective how they look for weaknesses to exploit.

---

[1] Please Download "Getting Your Hacking Lab Set Up at: http://www.concise-courses. com/learn/web-application-security/setup/

CHAPTER 1

Web Technologies

Note: Before starting Chapter 1, please download Lesson 0 (http://www.concise-courses. com/learn/web-application-security/setup/), which provides instructions on setting up your computer to perform the exercises in this book.

1.1 WEB SERVERS

The primary function of a web server is to store, process, and deliver web pages to clients. Client requests are processed by Hypertext Transfer Protocol (HTTP), the basic network protocol used to distribute information on the World Wide Web. Pages delivered are most frequently HTML documents that may include images, style sheets, and scripts, in addition to text content.

There is nothing mysterious about web servers, they work in a similar way to a file share on your Mac or Windows PC.

1.2 CLIENT-SIDE VERSUS SERVER-SIDE PROGRAMMING LANGUAGES

Web servers interpret some programming languages before presenting them to the user. These are called server-side programming languages. The developer writes the code for a web page, you as a web user request that page, and the server prepares that page, and then that content is sent to you through your web browser. Examples of server-side programming languages include: PHP, ASP, Python, and Java.

Client-side languages are different. Client-side languages are also code written by application developers. When a user requests a page, however, client-side languages are executed and interpreted by the user's browser, not by the web server. An example of a client-side language is JavaScript.

In summary, server-side languages are interpreted by the server, *before* actually getting to the user. Client-side languages are interpreted by the browser *after* they are sent to the user.

1.3 JAVASCRIPT – WHAT IS IT?

JavaScript executes in your browser, not on the server. That is an extremely important concept to remember. Generally, JavaScript is found between script tags (<script> </script>) on a page.

1.4 WHAT CAN JAVASCRIPT DO?

JavaScript is a powerful language because it can redirect and manipulate a user's browser: it can edit and change HTML on a page; it can change the look and feel of a page; change the style of a page; and it can log a user in and out of an application. Simply put, that which can be done in a browser can be done in JavaScript (and more!).

1.5 WHAT CAN JAVASCRIPT NOT DO?

JavaScript cannot directly interact with the server's file system because it is not running on the server; it is running in the browser. Therefore, JavaScript cannot make your browser send data from one domain to another; this is called cross-domain restrictions. In some special cases, this can be worked around, but in general it cannot, for example, transfer data from the web server hosting www.concise-courses.com to the web server hosting www.elsevier.com.

1.6 DATABASES

A database provides persistent data storage with quick access to that data. The most common ones are SQL (Structured Query Language) databases. SQL databases store data in tables and columns, and rows, and keys. Data is retrieved by using queries written in a structured syntax (hence the name). SQL syntax allows a website or a web application to retrieve, insert, and update records in a database.

1.7 WHAT ABOUT HTML?

HTML is a markup language that is generally static, and, with the adoption of HTML5, is getting more complicated and becoming a better attack surface.

1.8 WEB TECHNOLOGIES – PUTTING IT TOGETHER

The typical flow for a web application is the following: a user requests content (a webpage) through their web browser, and a web server serves that content via the folder that is shared with the world. The server-side scripting language is interpreted (PHP, ASP, Python, etc.) along with (possibly) data from a database, and the output is incorporated, and passed onto the user's browser. At the same time that the server-side content is received, the user's browser determines whether there is any client-side script, that is, code that is executed locally, typically JavaScript, Flash, or ActionScript. If there is, it executes it. The last step in this process is for the browser to render the end result, and the user is able to navigate the page.

1.9 DIGGING DEEPER

Most web application developers understand this workflow, but they do not always understand the technologies and protocols that power it. As hackers, we want to understand the application better than the people who built it, and then make it do what we want!

1.10 HYPERTEXT TRANSFER PROTOCOL (HTTP)

Hypertext Transfer Protocol (HTTP) is the language of the web and is what defines how browsers request and how servers receive content.

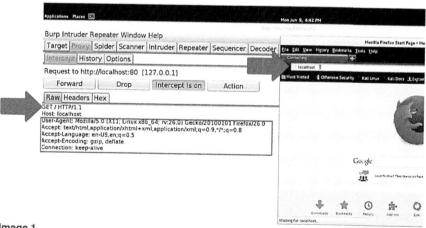

Image 1

Using a tool called Burp Suite, we can take a look at what an HTTP request looks like. We are going to open our browser and type "localhost" in the URL bar, which is going to connect to our local Linux machine (this can be any domain, such as google.com). Within Burp Suite we can see that the action we just took executes a GET request. This GET request (see the left arrow on Image 1) was generated by requesting the landing page of localhost (see the right arrow on Image 1).

We are going to use Burp Suite to start tweaking these raw requests, which we would normally not be able to do in a browser.

HTTP headers (see the box on Image 1) generally pass information from a browser to the web server of the web application. The user agent, for example, gives a web server information about yourself. In our example, you can see that we are running Firefox 26.0 and that we are using a 64-bit Linux machine, and so forth. The most important element to concentrate on is that HTTP headers all follow the same format. Referring to the image, think of the "Accept" statement as a "key" and the description as a "value," together forming a key-value pair that is being passed onto the web application (these are concepts familiar in programming).

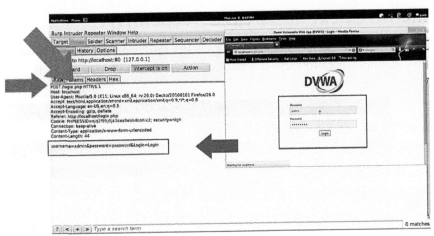

Image 2

That is a GET request, now let us look at POST requests. The POST request, in this example, is the result of logging into an application, the Damn Vulnerable Web Application (DVWA), specifically the "/login. php" page (see the left arrow in Image 2). We are posting data, giving information to the application to be used in some way, in this case the username and password to log in to the application (see the right arrow on Image 2).

There is the usual boilerplate information, for example the HTTP 1.1 protocol (see diagonal arrow on Image 2) and the host information, localhost. The data in the box of the image is another set of key-value pairs, the username "key" has the "value" of "admin" and the password "key" has the "value" of "password."

In summary, POST requests are meant to pass data *to* an application, such as a login, username, and password, whereas GET requests are meant to request data *from* the web application.

1.11 VERBS

GET and POST are called verbs. As we saw, GET requests pass information via the URL using a parameter in the URL. POST requests pass information via their own parameters, but they are not visible in the URL. It can be confusing that both GET and POST requests can pass information to the application, but these two actions are meant for different purposes. Typically, POST requests are used for sensitive data such as usernames and passwords, so they are not visible in the URL. Developers, however, tend to use one or the other interchangeably.

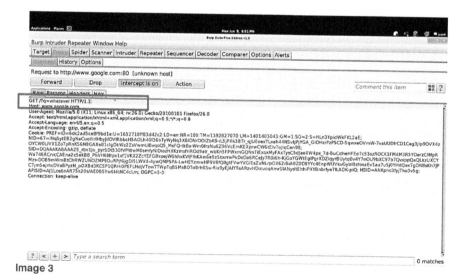

Image 3

For this next example I am sending a GET request to google.com with the "q = whatever" parameter attached to it, (refer to the box in Image 3). This is going to tell Google that the search query (q) that "I want to use the word 'whatever' in my search request."

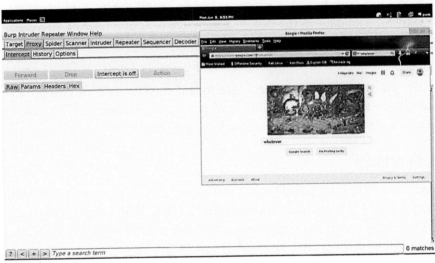

Image 4

Image 4 shows what this search query looks like in a browser. I am passing in "q = whatever" into the URL bar which auto-populates "whatever" into the search bar, and now I can conduct a Google search on that word.

1.12 SPECIAL CHARACTERS AND ENCODINGS

URL percent encoding is used to pass special HTTP characters through the HTTP protocol safely when using GET and POST parameters. The reason for encoding is that some characters have special meanings in HTTP. Special characters in HTTP include things like line breaks, spaces, and so forth.

1.13 COOKIES, SESSIONS, AND AUTHENTICATION

The HTTP protocol does not know some important things like whether we are a specific user, or if we are allowed to be on a certain page. To assist with this, applications issue cookies, and session tokens to keep track of what a user has or has not done on the application, for example logging in.

Cookies and session tokens are values passed along in HTTP requests marking that a user has performed a certain action already. Cookies might persist if they are stored in a web browser, but session tokens are generally removed after a browsing session is complete.

1.14 SHORT EXERCISE: LINUX MACHINE SETUP

Our first exercise is to get Burp Suite up and running[1], and to allow traffic to flow through it. Burp Suite is our main attack and reconnaissance tool, you have already seen it in action in several of the previous examples.

In Image 5 you can see we are in our terminal, in the tools directory, where we have already downloaded the .jar file for Burp Suite. To open the tool we simply type in the terminal:

java – jar burpsuite_free_v1.5.jar

Press Enter, and Burp Suite will automatically open.

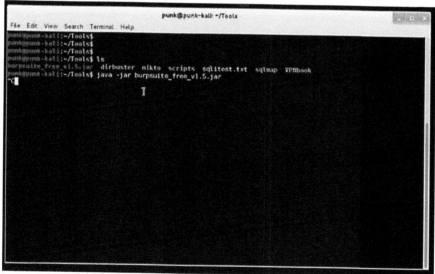

Image 5

Further, let us open our web browser and configure it to use Burp Suite. Navigate to Firefox > Preferences > Advanced > Network Tab.

---

[1] Please Download "Getting Your Hacking Lab Set Up at: http://www.concise-courses.com/learn/web-application-security/setup/

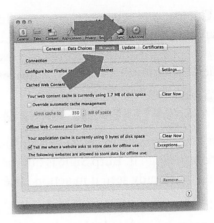

Image 6

A default setup will state "No proxy," we need to change this to "Manual proxy configuration." In the HTTP proxy field enter "127. 0.0.1" (your local IP) and Port 8080.

Make sure that the "No proxy for" field is completely empty.

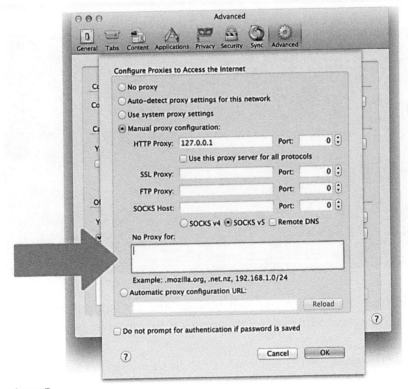

Image 7

You can leave all other settings as they are. Your browser is now configured to use Burp Suite.

1.15 USING THE BURP SUITE INTERCEPTING PROXY

Burp Suite is a fully featured web application attack tool: it does almost anything that you could ever want to do when penetration testing a web application.

One of Burp Suite's main features is its ability to intercept HTTP requests. Normally HTTP requests go from your browser straight to a web server and then the web server response is sent back to your browser. With Burp Suite, however, HTTP requests go from your browser straight to Burp Suite, which intercepts the traffic.

In Burp Suite you can then tweak the raw HTTP in various ways before forwarding the request on to the web server. Essentially this tool is acting as a proxy, a "man in the middle," between you and the web application, allowing you to have finer control over the exact traffic you are sending and receiving.

Our goal with the Burp intercepting proxy feature is to tweak requests so they still follow the rules of HTTP, but can make the application act unexpectedly.

1.16 WHY IS THE INTERCEPTING PROXY IMPORTANT?

Your browser constrains your interaction with web applications by only allowing very specific HTTP requests. Using client or server-side programming and code, the HTTP requests are directed to you by the website developer. A website developer, for example, might have written a contact form on a page that will constrain the HTTP traffic by limiting what you can enter into the form. Burp Suite allows you to break free from the browser and web application and tweak the raw HTTP request so you can send any traffic that you want: *this is very important to remember*.

In the following examples you will see many references to the intercept feature. An important element to note here is that if you find yourself trying to use your browser later and it appears to be frozen, or takes a very long time to load, check to make sure that you have not left "Intercept" on in Burp Suite.

1.17 SHORT EXERCISE – USING THE BURP SUITE DECODER

The goal of this exercise is to understand and tweak an HTTP request and properly encode characters within the HTTP protocol so that the reflected page outputs a "+" sign.

Exercise steps:

1. Login to the DVWA and go to the XSS Reflected page.
2. The first step in understanding how to hack a website is to understand how a normal user would use the website. For example, you might enter your name and you receive an "echo" or reply back with a "hello" in front of it.

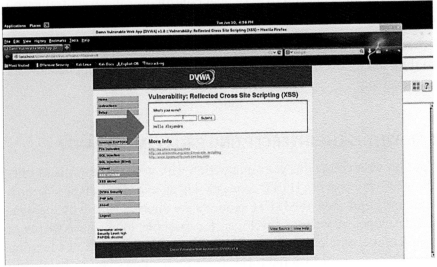

Image 8

3. Now you want to intercept that request, so go to Burp Suite, hit the Proxy tab and turn "Intercept" on.

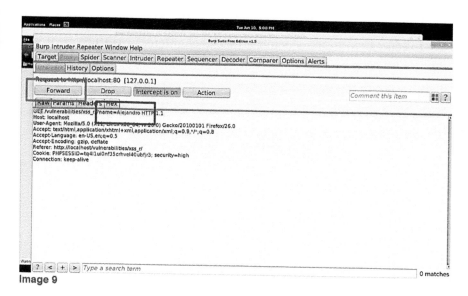
Image 9

4. Back in DVWA, enter your name in the text box and hit Submit again. Go back to Burp Suite and you can see that it has captured the HTTP request – it is a GET request, submitting a parameter called "name" with the value that you entered, in our example "Alejandro" (see bottom box in Image 9).
5. Now forward the request on to the web server by hitting "Forward" (see the top box Image 9). Back in DVWA you will see it echoing the name you entered.

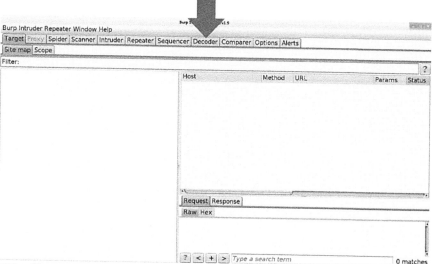
Image 10

Now we want to understand HTTP encoding, so we will try to get the page to echo a "+" sign, which is a special character in HTTP.

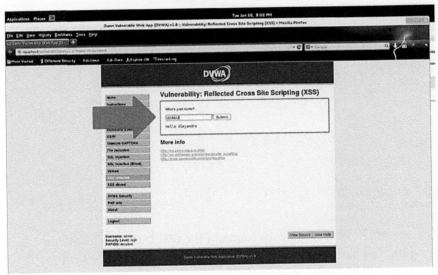

Image 11

1. Go back to the DVWA and submit something random so it can be intercepted (see arrow in Image 11).

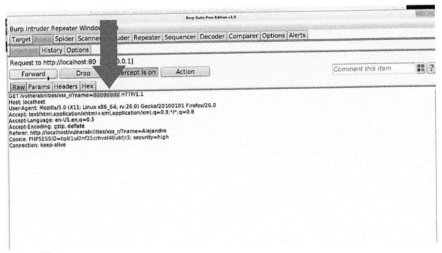

Image 12

2. Go to the intercepted HTTP request in Burp Suite. We see that all Burp Suite is doing is echoing back whatever you type in to the value of this parameter. If you were to forward this, it would say "hello dddddddd" (See arrow in Image 12).

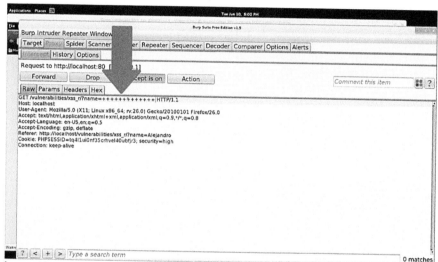

Image 13

3. Enter several "+" signs in place of your name, (so it reads "name = ++ + + + +"), and hit "Forward" (see arrow in Image 13).

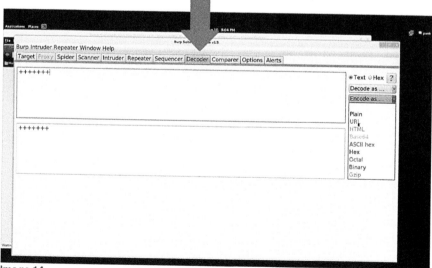

Image 14

4. Back in the DVWA you will see that there is no output for your name – why not? Well, "+" is a special character in HTTP, it indicates a space. A literal space would break the HTTP protocol, so it needs to be represented by something, and that something is the "+." In order to get the web application to echo this symbol, we have to do something special.

5. Go back and repeat steps 1–3, but this time, instead of just entering the "+" symbols into the raw HTTP request, enter them into the Decoder tab of Burp Suite.

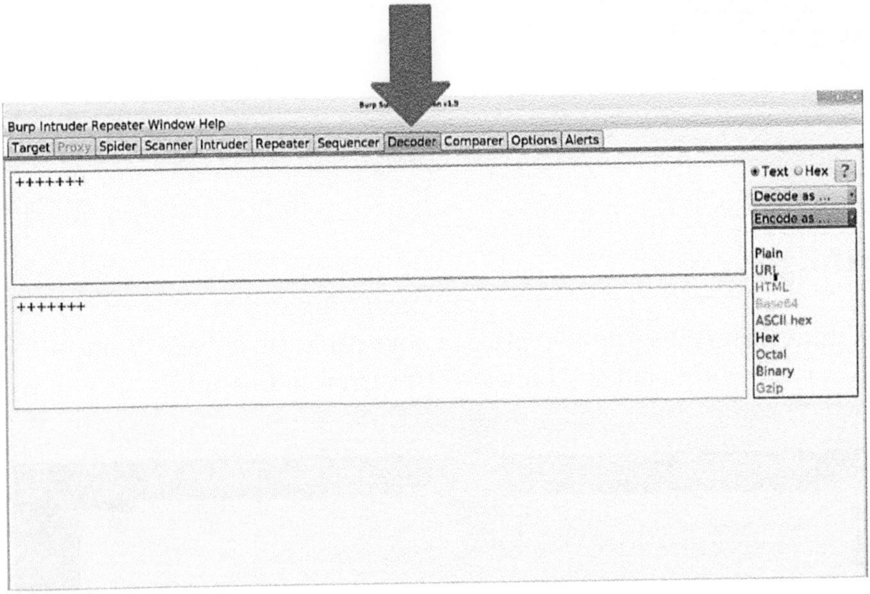

Image 15

6. Here we can encode this string as a URL. In the "Encode as" dropdown on the right select URL (see Image 15). This will translate the "+" sign so that when it passes the string to the application it will be interpreted as the literal "+" sign, not a space.

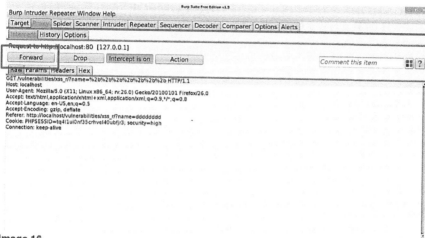

Image 16

7. Copy-paste the URL-encoded string from the Decoder tab into your raw HTTP request in the "name =" field. Then forward that along to the application and you will see your string of "+" signs echoed into the application.

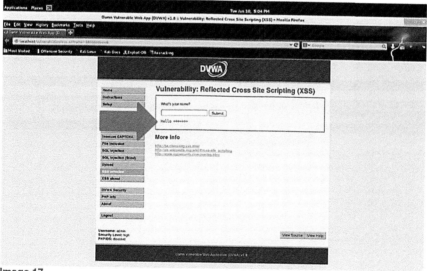

Image 17

Hopefully after this exercise you have a good idea of how to use Burp Suite as an intercepting proxy and how to tweak the raw HTTP request and encode special characters.

1.18 SHORT EXERCISE – GETTING COMFORTABLE WITH HTTP AND BURP SUITE

The goal of this exercise is to get comfortable with how HTTP passes information to an application.

Exercise steps:

1. Your Burp Suite interception proxy should be set to "Intercept Off."
2. Open up DVWA, login, and go to the Command Execution page.
3. Enter an IP address in the box (you can just use 127.0.0.1) and check out the functionality.
4. Now turn "Intercept On" and go through the same process.

Answer the following questions:

- Is this using a POST or GET request to pass information?
- What else might this application be interacting with? (A database? Client-side scripts? The underlying operating system?)
- Is the DVWA using a cookie? If so, what for?

Go to the XSS Stored page of DVWA, repeat the process, and answer the same questions.

1.18.1 Solution

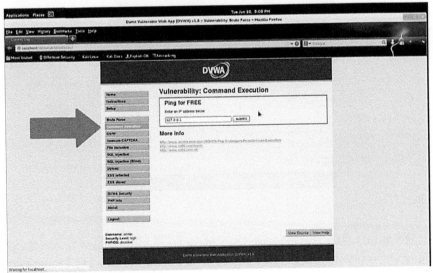

Image 18

The first step is to understand what this application is trying to do for a typical user. So, on the Command Execution page, enter the loopback address, 127.0.0.1, submit it, and see what happens.

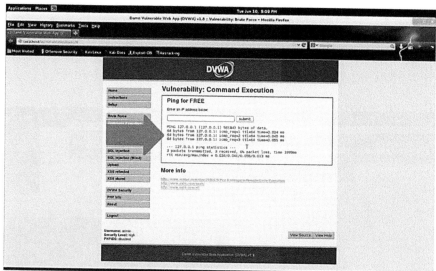

Image 19

The web application is pinging that IP address, which sends a request to that IP and waits for a response to see if that host is "alive." We see the results of the pings, telling us that the packet (the "ping") is transmitted and received, with 0% packet loss, meaning the host is alive.

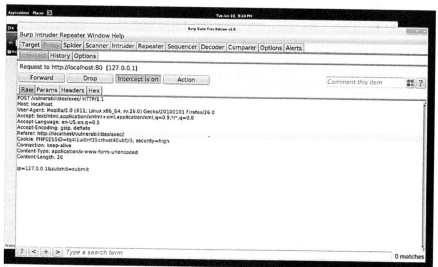

Image 20

Now we will use Burp Suite to examine this traffic to better understand it.

Looking at the captured request, we notice that it is POSTing some information to/vulnerabilities/exec, so the answer to the first question is that the application is using a POST request.

We also see that it is passing the IP address in two parameters, "ip = 127.0.0.1&submit = submit" which is all very standard.

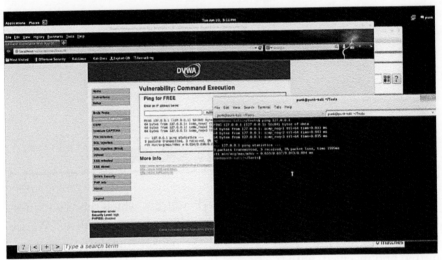

Image 21

Those familiar with Linux will understand the output in Image 21, but now let us see what happens when we ping 127.0.0.1 in the terminal. That output is almost exactly the same as what we see in the application. That tells us that this application is using the underlying operating system to perform a ping, and then give us back those results. All it is doing is submitting whatever IP you enter into the box into the ping command in your terminal, and then taking that output and dumping it to the application. The answer to the next question, therefore, is that it is interacting with the underlying operating system.

In terms of the actual workflow of the page, we enter an IP address that is submitted via a POST request, that information is sent to our underlying operating system, which performs a ping, then the application grabs that output and dumps it to the page.

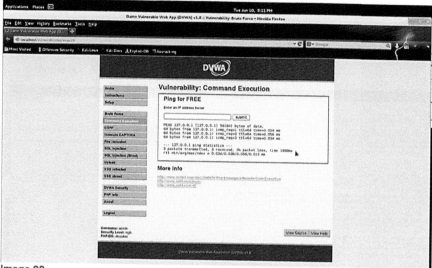

Image 22

Now let us look at the XSS Stored page, which is a dummy guest book-signing page. As a first step, try to use it as a normal user to get a general feel of how the application works. We notice that our name and message is stored on the page as soon as we click "Sign Guestbook."

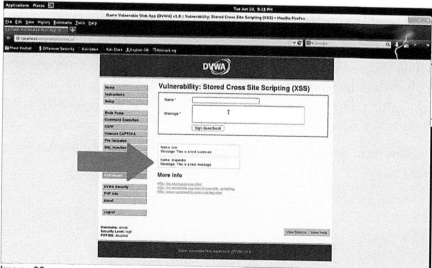

Image 23

Back in Burp Suite turn "Intercept On" and see what happens when we enter a different message.

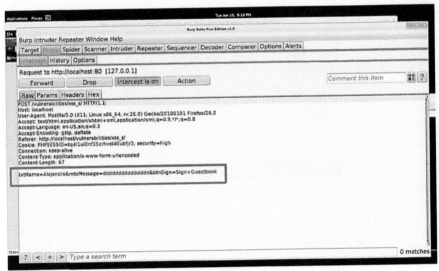

Image 24

We can see that it is using a **POST** request to/vulnerabilities/xss_s and submitting our information through these two parameters: "TxtName" and "MtxMessage" (refer to box on Image 24).

We can reason that there must be some sort of persistent storage within this application because the name and message are persistently available on the page – if you reload the page you will see that information again, it does not go away. Because the information is persistent, we know that it must be stored in a database.

Now turn "Intercept Off" in Burp Suite and refresh the DVWA page (see Image 25).

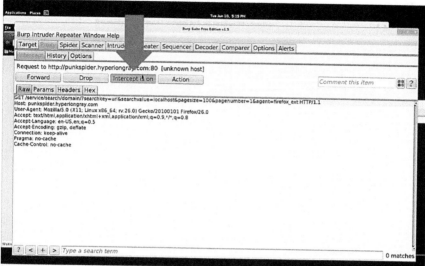

Image 25

You will see that the messages have persisted on the page (see Image 26).

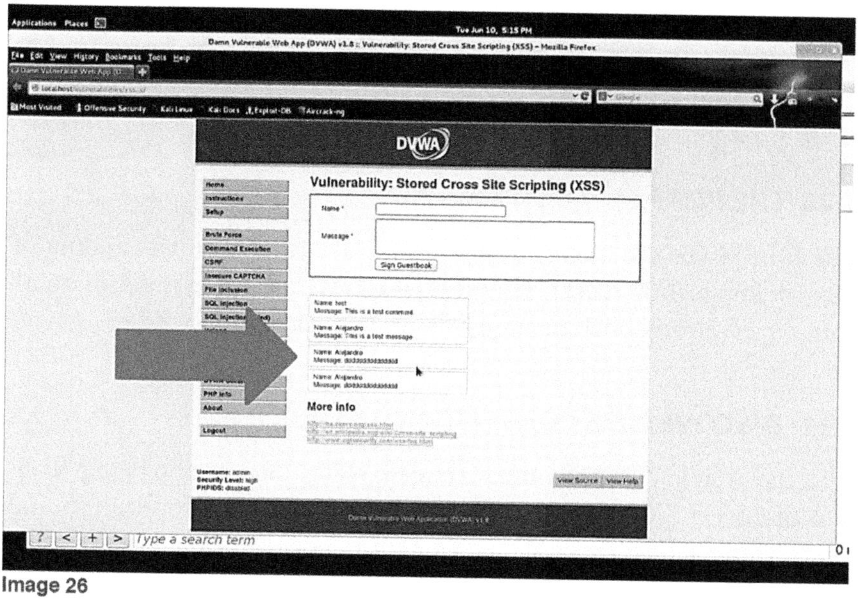

Image 26

Remember that we mentioned SQL previously – to retrieve information from the database the application must be executing SQL query, or command.

To recap, the workflow of this page is: a user enters a name and a message, which gets passed as a POST request, and the information is stored into the database and retrieved via a SQL command each time that page is loaded.

1.19 UNDERSTANDING THE APPLICATION

Our goal in this section is to understand how an application works.

We need to ask the following questions:

- What technologies is an application using?
- Is there anything obviously dangerous going on in the application?
- How does the application pass data back and forth? What are some of the places where user input is being passed?
- Where is the database being queried? Is user input being used here to actually query the database?
- Where is the application displaying user-supplied input?
- Where is user-supplied input actually being printed to the page? (Printed data on a page is something that can often times be very dangerous because it is a significant cause of bugs in a website).

1.20 THE BURP SUITE SITE MAP

The Burp Suite site map is going to give us a better understanding of how an application works. It is always a great idea to take notes on all your observations when playing with an application.

1.21 DISCOVERING CONTENT AND STRUCTURES

Effective web hacking is quite formulaic, with the first step being "content discovery." Click on absolutely everything in an application and monitor the HTTP requests to understand how the data is being used. This can be a monumental task, especially for a large website, or application, but you can use the Burp Suite Spider to help you.

1.22 UNDERSTANDING AN APPLICATION

Patience is paramount when trying to understand an application. If you discover technologies that you do not understand, search online for more information. Googling HTTP requests, for example, is a fast, simple, and effective way to learn what they are doing.

CHAPTER 2

Exploitation

Let us look at the Burp Suite site map and Spider.

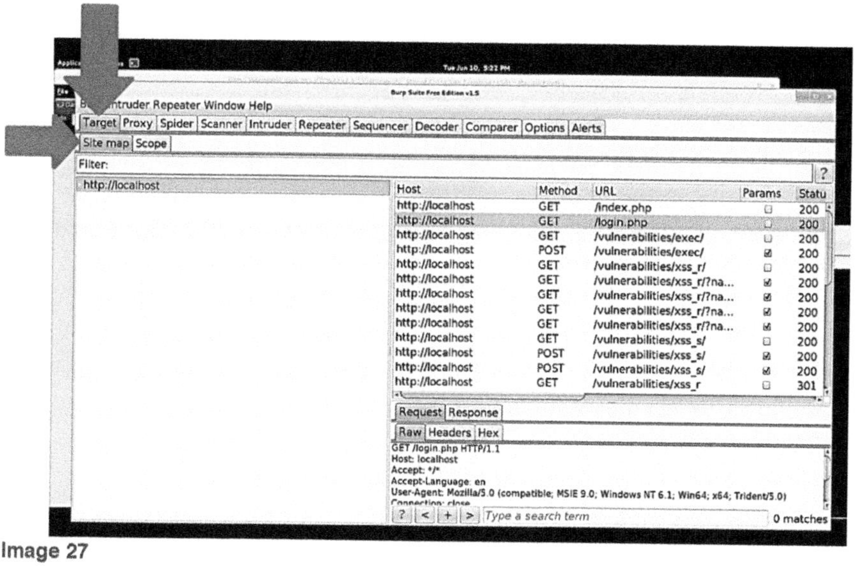

Image 27

Within Burp Suite we have selected the "Target" tab and then the "Sitemap" (see Image 27).

What you see is a list of the targets that Burp Suite will automatically pick up as you browse around the web. Burp Suite automatically maps out websites and presents them in an intuitive way for you – how nice! The first thing you see in our example is just the localhost since we have only visited Damn Vulnerable Web App (DVWA) so far, which is on our local machine (see the box in Image 28).

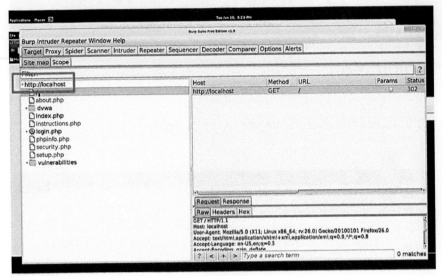

Image 28

If we double click on the localhost target, you can see the webroot that shows us the request that we generated when we navigated to the DVWA in the browser.

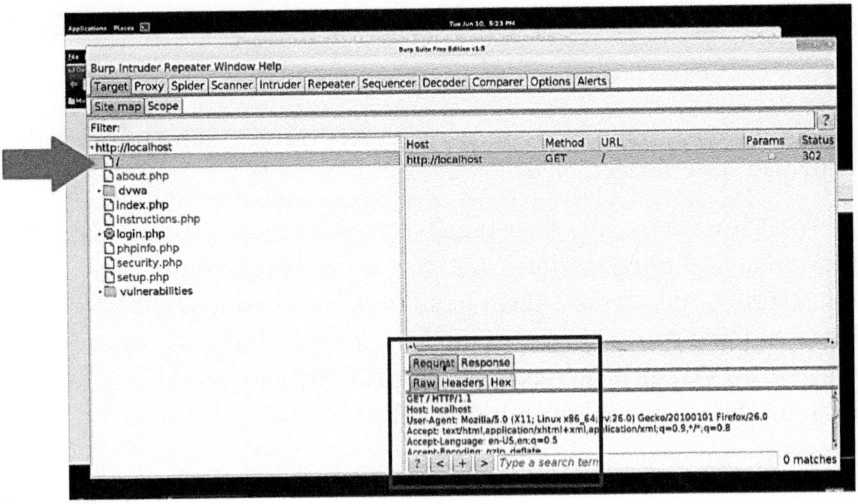

Image 29

We can see the HTTP request that was sent when we navigated to DVWA in our web browser. We have tabs for viewing the raw HTTP requests and the responses, as well as the headers (see box in Image 29).

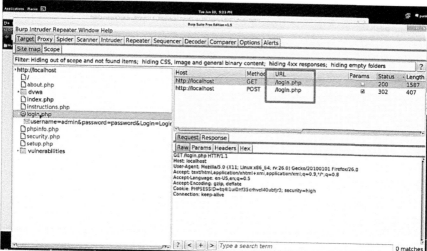

Image 30

In this image, you can see how Burp Suite maps out the application for us, showing us that there are folders called about.php, index.php, instructions.php, login.php, and so forth. (see the box in Image 30).

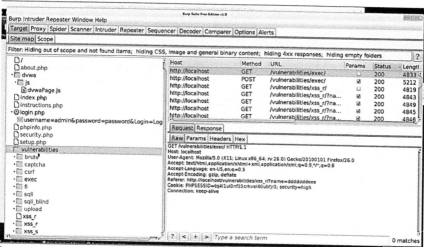

Image 31

In the "vulnerabilities" folder, you can see all the requests we made to the various pages of the DVWA application in our earlier exercises.

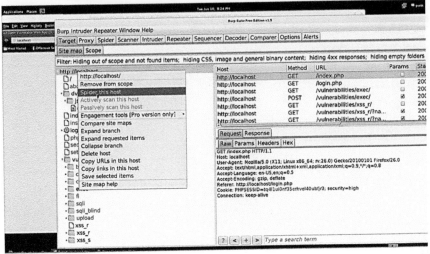

Image 32

When you right-click on any of these folders or on the root, you can select to "Spider This Host" that helps to discover additional content or "Spider This Branch," which will constrain the spider to specific branches, or subfolders.

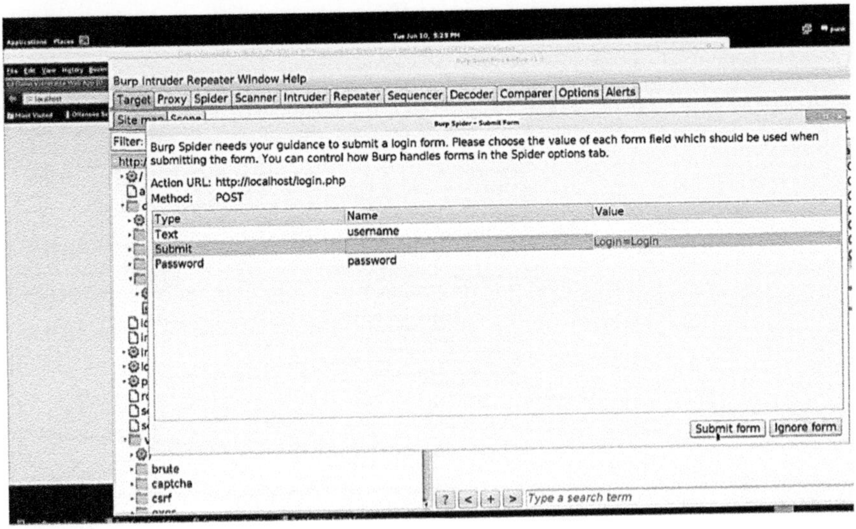

Image 33

If we select to "Spider the Host" at the root level, we notice that it automatically detects form submissions and lets us provide information for the spider to input into the form, for example, a username and password (see Image 33). The Burp Suite Spider tool is quite useful.

2.1 BYPASSING CLIENT SIDE CONTROLS

The first exploit that we will examine is being able to bypass client-side controls, which as we mentioned earlier are constraints on the information that your browser is allowed to pass to the application. Developers have a misconceived notion that they control the data that comes from your browser. As a user you are always in control of everything that comes from your machine: you just need to learn *how*.

2.1.1 Steps for Bypassing Controls
1. Look for places where client-side controls are being used.
2. Look for disabled check boxes, disabled radio buttons, check parameters in POST and GET requests that look unsafe.
3. Use the Burp Suite intercepting proxy to capture requests and analyze GET and POST request parameters. Use context clues to understand what these parameters are actually for. Developers typically try to develop things such that when they debug them, they can look at the code and understand what it is doing. Therefore, developers typically do not create GET and POST parameters that are just a random series of strings and numbers, because they will not know what these things mean when they go to debug the application. They are usually given some kind of a logical name. So we can try to understand what that name is, what the parameter is doing for the web application and what kind of data it is passing.
4. Look for parameters that appear to be unsafe, tweak them, and see what happens. If, for example, there is a debug parameter being passed through a POST request and it says "debug = off," see what happens if you change it to "debug = on." The application might give you additional data on what it is doing and provide you with additional information that can be used to plan an attack.
5. Rinse and repeat. Do this for every GET and POST parameter in the web application to allow you to see what each link and each page is doing.

2.2 BYPASSING CLIENT-SIDE CONTROLS – EXAMPLE

Here is an example of a client-side control, which is using JavaScript for form validation.

Image 34

Visit http://course.hyperiongray.com to access this exercise and click on "client-example" (see Image 34).

Like always, the first thing to do is to behave like a normal user to see how a web application functions normally, so once you have clicked the "client-example" link, just pretend you are a normal user and enter your zip code. If we enter 22222 as our zip code, we notice that the application prints "thank you, your zip code has been entered as: 22222."

We notice that we are unable to enter more than five characters because zip codes in the United States are limited by five characters. Now let us see if we can hack this. The first check is to view the source code of the page (in Firefox, right-click and select "View Page Source").

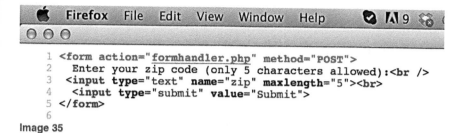

```
1  <form action="formhandler.php" method="POST">
2    Enter your zip code (only 5 characters allowed):<br />
3    <input type="text" name="zip" maxlength="5"><br>
4      <input type="submit" value="Submit">
5  </form>
6
```

Image 35

The page source code tells us that it is limiting the maximum length attribute in the input to five characters. My browser, not the web server, is therefore preventing me from entering more than five characters, which means there is an opportunity to bypass client-side controls.

Let us see what the request looks like through Burp Suite by entering my zip code as 66666.

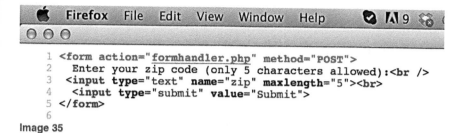

Image 36

We notice that the application is sending a POST request to "client-example/formhandler.php" (see the top box in Image 36).

At the bottom, we can see the actual POST data, the data that has been passed to the web application. As mentioned before, GET requests are actually visible in the URL, however, POST requests are not (see the bottom box in Image 36). The zip-code data is being passed through the "zip" POST parameter so let us forward it along and see what the web application does under normal conditions.

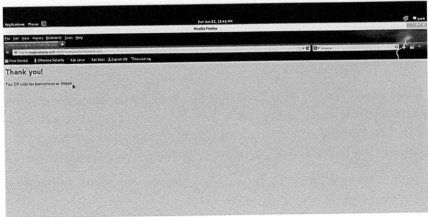

Image 37

Since we entered "66666" in the zip parameter, it prints the same on the page (see Image 37).

Now that we have discovered the raw HTTP request, we have total freedom – we have "broken out" of the browser and what the application developer has permitted us to do. Try passing a string longer than five characters and see what happens (see the box in Image 38).

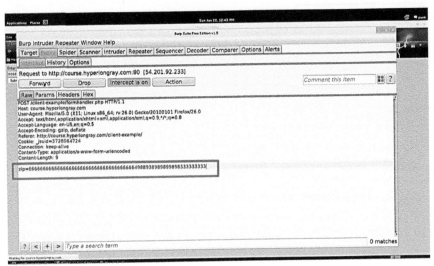

Image 38

There are additional things that you could do with this, just do not forget to percentage encode your text before inserting it into the HTTP request.

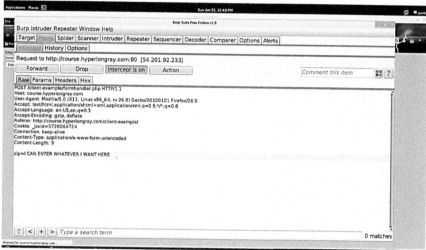
Image 39

2.2.1 Short Exercise: Bypassing Client-Side Control
Goal: Buy a movie for $0.01

1. Go to http://course.hyperiongray.com
2. Click on the "client" folder. Explore the application, understand it, and see how it is passing data. Identify if anything looks suspicious or hackable.

As you probably figured out, this application is a movie-buying application. Your goal is to pick a movie from the list and try to buy it for one cent. Do not worry, this is a dummy site that we created for this book, you will not actually be purchasing anything.

2.3 BYPASSING CLIENT-SIDE CONTROLS – EXERCISE SOLUTION

As always, first behave like a normal user to see how things work. For this example, I selected to buy "Big Momma's House" for $10.99.

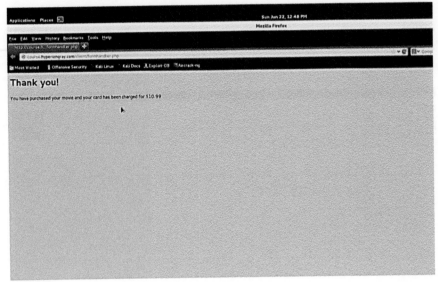

Image 40

Now take a look using Burp Suite – turn "Intercept On," click "buy" and take a look at the raw requests.

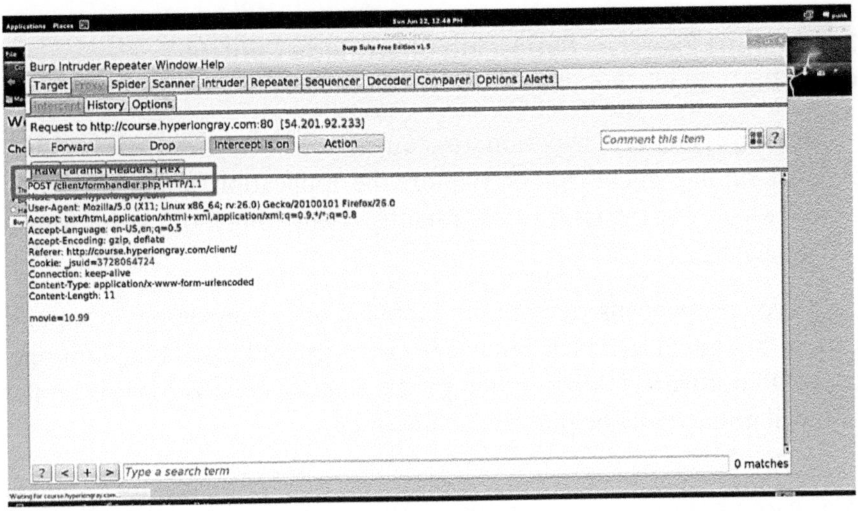

Image 41

This is a very similar to the last example, we can see that it is POSTing to "/client/formhandler.php" (see the box in Image 41). We can also see that the host is "course/hyperiongray.com," which is useful information.

We see that it is passing the price of the movie as $10.99 within a POST parameter. This is a huge vulnerability because a hacker can potentially manipulate the price.

Edit the HTTP request and enter $0.01 as the price. Forward the request on, and you will see that you have complete control over the price just by being able to edit the raw HTTP request.

2.4 SQL INJECTION

SQL injection is a very common vulnerability.

As we learned earlier, SQL is an abbreviation for "Structured Query Language." Typically a server-side language (like SQL) will build the query and execute it on the server and database to return useful data.

Here is a quick example of SQL working:

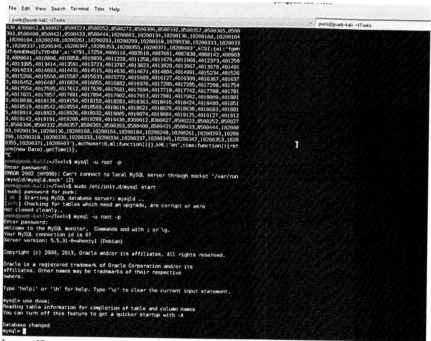

Image 42

In a terminal, we have opened a MySQL shell and connected to the DVWA database, which is a MySQL database, one of the most common types of SQL databases used on the web. The MySQL shell allows me to navigate the database easily.

Image 43

I typed the "Show Tables" command that lists the tables stored with the DVWA database.

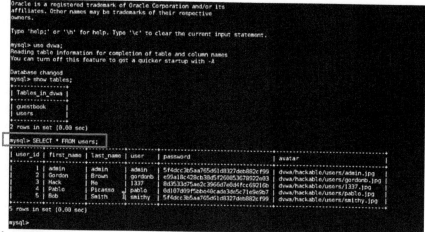

Image 44

Next, I am telling the database to give me all the data from the Users table with the command

*mysql>SELECT * FROM users*

(see the box in Image 44).

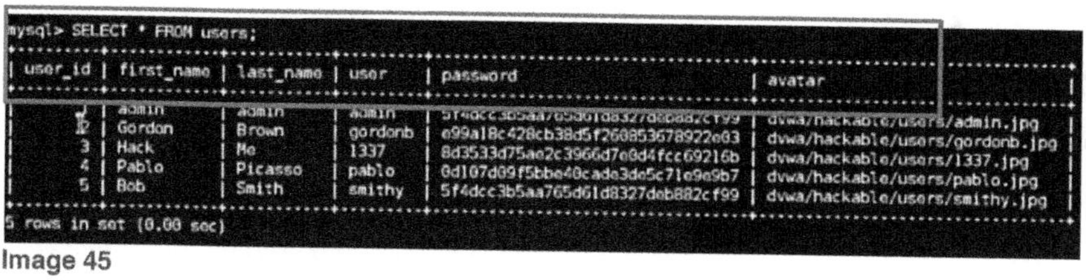

Image 45

SQL stores data in columns and rows. You can see a series of columns, that is, User ID, First Name, Last Name, User, Password, Avatar, and so forth with unique entries listed in the rows (see box in Image 45).

Notice that the password is not the actual password but a hash of the password. Hashing is a one-way algorithm that converts the password to an encoded value. This is used so that if a hacker steals the database they would not know the users' passwords, because (in theory) you cannot un-hash a hashed password.

```
mysql> use dvwa;
Reading table information for completion of table and column names
You can turn off this feature to get a quicker startup with -A

Database changed
mysql> show tables;
+----------------+
| Tables_in_dvwa |
+----------------+
| guestbook      |
| users          |
+----------------+
2 rows in set (0.00 sec)

mysql> SELECT * FROM users;
+---------+------------+-----------+---------+----------------------------------+-------------------------------------+
| user_id | first_name | last_name | user    | password                         | avatar                              |
+---------+------------+-----------+---------+----------------------------------+-------------------------------------+
|       1 | admin      | admin     | admin   | 5f4dcc3b5aa765d61d8327deb882cf99 | dvwa/hackable/users/admin.jpg       |
|       2 | Gordon     | Brown     | gordonb | e99a18c428cb38d5f260853678922e03 | dvwa/hackable/users/gordonb.jpg     |
|       3 | Hack       | Me        | 1337    | 8d3533d75ae2c3966d7e8d4fcc6921b  | dvwa/hackable/users/1337.jpg        |
|       4 | Pablo      | Picasso   | pablo   | 0d107d09f5bbe40cade3de5c71e9e9b7 | dvwa/hackable/users/pablo.jpg       |
|       5 | Bob        | Smith     | smithy  | 5f4dcc3b5aa765d61d8327deb882cf99 | dvwa/hackable/users/smithy.jpg      |
+---------+------------+-----------+---------+----------------------------------+-------------------------------------+
5 rows in set (0.00 sec)

mysql> SELECT first_name,last_name FROM users;
+------------+-----------+
| first_name | last_name |
+------------+-----------+
| admin      | admin     |
| Gordon     | Brown     |
| Hack       | Me        |
| Pablo      | Picasso   |
| Bob        | Smith     |
+------------+-----------+
5 rows in set (0.00 sec)

mysql>
```

Image 46

2.5 SQL INJECTION

SQL injection is all about syntax. As we have discovered, if we take the following SQL normal query,

SELECT first_name, last_name FROM users WHERE user_id= '1'

…this would return rows stored in the Users table for the user where user_id is 1.

(see the box in Image 47)

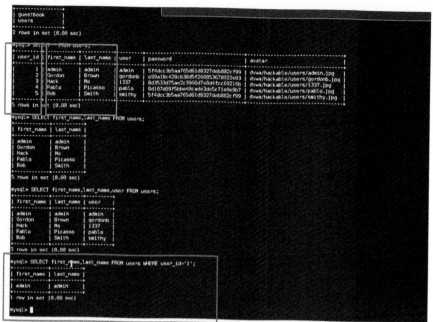

Image 47

Exactly the same is applicable to user_id=2. In our example, user_id=2 would be "Gordon" and "Brown" – see the box in Image 47.

PHP (server-side language) passes the SQL commands as strings. PHP stores the query as a piece of text that the application can use when it is passed to the backend database – but there is a disconnect here. The server-side language has no context as to what the user is asking for. It is just passing a "dumb" piece of text. This is an important concept to understand.

Let us say the user is given the ability to enter whatever user_id that they want in the above query, and they decide to enter "1" or "1"="1" – what is that going to do to the query? For example:

*SELECT * FROM users WHERE user_id= '1' OR '1'='1'*

The above syntax tells the application to get all of the rows from the database where the user_id is 1 or where 1 = 1. Since 1 always equals 1, this is going to return the First_Name and Last_Name records of everybody in the users table. Essentially, what we have done is messed with the logic of the query, simply by entering some unusual syntax.

```
+--------------+-----------+
| first_name | last_name |
+--------------+-----------+
| admin      | admin     |
+--------------+-----------+
1 row in set (0.00 sec)

mysql> SELECT first_name,last_name FROM users WHERE user_id='2';
+--------------+-----------+
| first_name | last_name |
+--------------+-----------+
| Gordon     | Brown     |
+--------------+-----------+
1 row in set (0.00 sec)

mysql> SELECT first_name,last_name FROM users WHERE user_id='1';
+--------------+-----------+
| first_name | last_name |
+--------------+-----------+
| admin      | admin     |
+--------------+-----------+
1 row in set (0.00 sec)

mysql> SELECT first_name,last_name FROM users WHERE user_id='1' OR '1'='1';
+--------------+-----------+
| first_name | last_name |
+--------------+-----------+
| admin      | admin     |
| Gordon     | Brown     |
| Hack       | Me        |
| Pablo      | Picasso   |
| Bob        | Smith     |
+--------------+-----------+
5 rows in set (0.00 sec)

mysql>
```

Image 48

You might be asking yourself, how do I actually open a SQL shell? That is an important question!

The real answer is that you do not. You will not need to work in a SQL shell. Unless a web application is *really* bad, you will not have access to the backend database nor an SQL shell. You will not be able to see the database or navigate around it as we have been doing in the above examples.

All you are going to see is the web application, and from here you need to figure out how to inject and form your syntax in a way that makes the application do something unexpected.

Let us look at an example of that right now.

Back in the DVWA application on the SQL Injection page, it asks me for a User ID. The first step as always is to treat the application like a normal user (have we repeated this enough yet?).

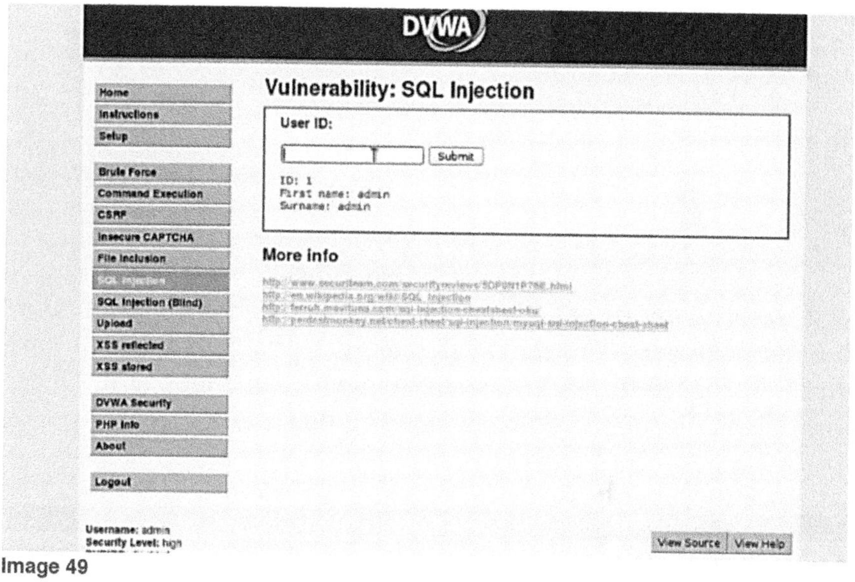

Image 49

As you can see in Image 49, if I enter the user ID of 1 and you see that it prints "First name: admin" and "Surname: admin."

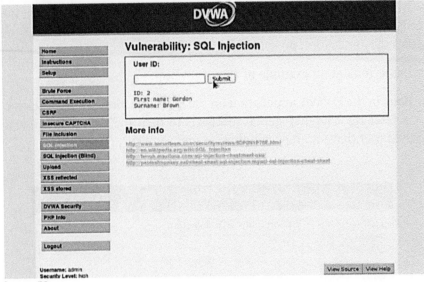

Image 50

If we put a user ID of 2, then we see that the database spits out "Gordon" and "Brown". This should all look somewhat familiar as we have already navigated the backend database and taken a look at it. Under normal conditions you would not have had that luxury.

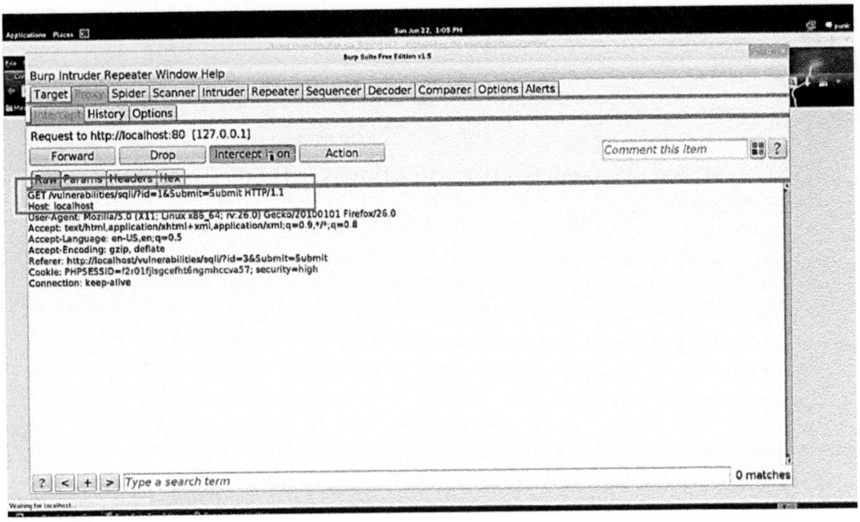

Image 51

Let us see what this looks like in Burp Suite. Turn "Intercept On" and enter the User ID as 1 again.

In Burp Suite, we see that it is conducting a GET request to "/vulnerabilities/sqli" and you see that the "ID" and "Submit" are passed over in parameters (see the box in Image 51). Another thing to notice is that security is set to "high."

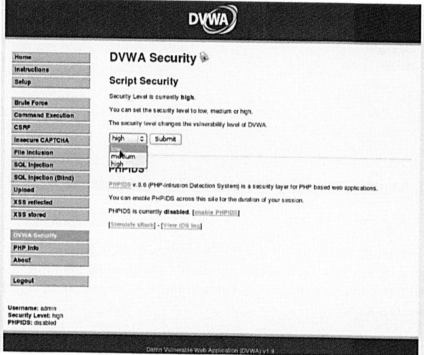

Image 52

Before we continue this exercise, we want to turn the security to "low" in DVWA. Once we are elite hackers, we can turn it up to "high."

Going back to the SQL injection example, we need to identify if there is a SQL injection possibility or not, so let us throw unusual SQL syntax at it and see what happens.

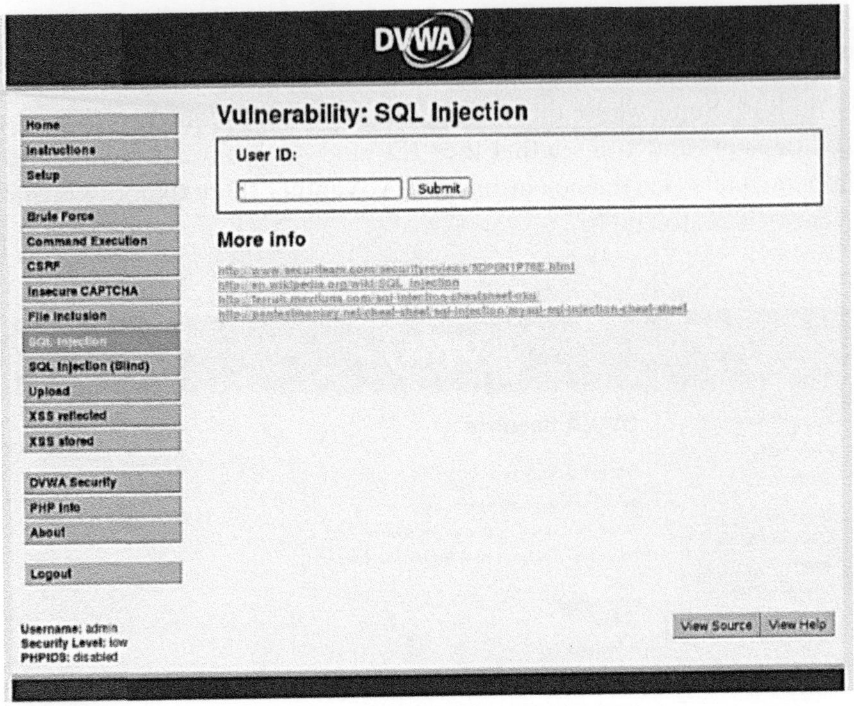

Image 53

Typically an apostrophe is a good way to test for SQL injection. When we were in a SQL shell we used apostrophes to surround the strings we want to give to the application. Let us see what happens if we enter just an apostrophe.

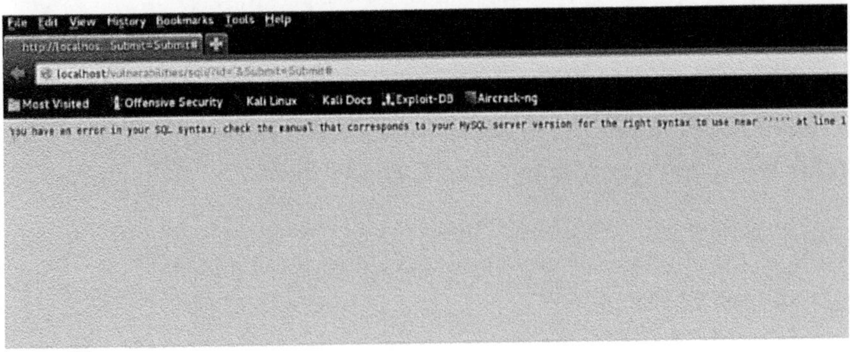

Image 54

We see a very common error: you have an error in your SQL syntax (see Image 54). Now 99.9% of the time I know that this means the application is vulnerable to SQL injection. We will talk a little bit more about finding vulnerabilities later, but all you need to know for now is that I put an apostrophe, it broke the SQL syntax, which means that I can edit that syntax.

Armed with the knowledge that the SQL syntax can be broken, we can now predict user_id's and request other such data.

Image 55

So, let us try this:

SELECT firstname,surname FROM users WHERE id='1'

The above is very typical since the table users is often called "users." So, let us mess with the logic while not actually breaking the syntax. To achieve this, let us see what happens if we input an apostrophe that does not always break the syntax but can produce interesting results. We know that the query is going to be passed with an opening and closing apostrophe. So, let us alter the syntax assuming that these apostrophes will be added by the web application, so it looks like this:

SELECT firstname,surname FROM users WHERE id=1' OR '1'='1

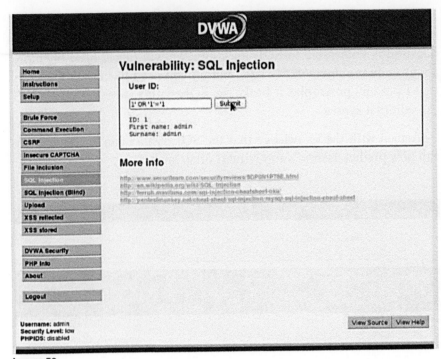

Image 56

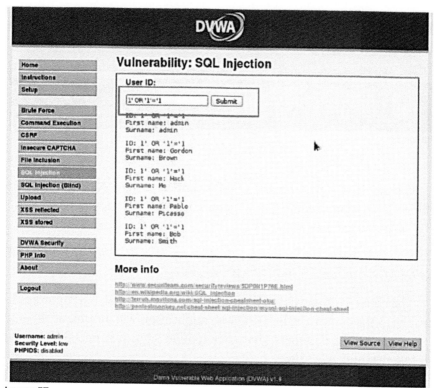

Image 57

In the example, we can see some unexpected results. What this should do is print out every first name and last name (see the box in Image 57).

It does in fact give me every first name and last name, and the reason it does that is because of the "1=1" statement. We have now established arbitrary access to the backend database.

This next part is going to get a little bit complicated in that you need to know SQL syntax to perform the next hack, which is to steal the database.

Image 58

Having used SQL for many years, I know that the UNION statement allows me to concatenate data together. I know that instead of entering "1," I can do the following:

SELECT firstname,surname FROM users WHERE id='1' UNION SELECT user,password FROM users#'

The above syntax will break something because there is a rogue apostrophe at the end of the line (the web application will automatically put it there), but the comment character (pound sign) instructs SQL to ignore everything after the #.

This syntax instructs SQL to give me the users and passwords from the users table and combine it with the data that was previously given to me. Entering the above string in DVWA gives me the following:

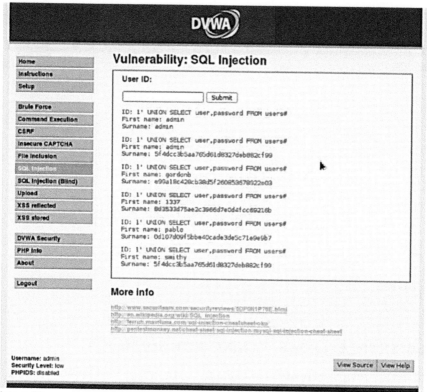

Image 59

As we can see we have broken the web application. The first record is "admin admin," which is expected, because we entered a command requesting the first record, id="1."

I also requested other users and passwords from the users table that generated the hashed passwords within the surname field.

We mentioned that hashed passwords cannot, in theory, be un-hashed, but people have generated hashes for many common passwords and posted them online, so you can often simply Google hashed passwords to obtain the un-hashed version.

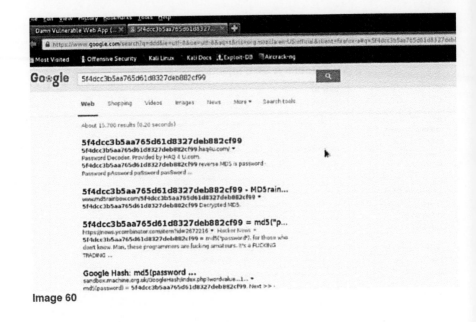

Image 60

2.6 SHORT EXERCISE: PWNING WITH SQLMap

The goal of this exercise is to steal a username/password combo (besides admin/password) and login to the DVWA as another user.

We have looked at the manual (and complicated) way of SQL injection. The good news is that there are automatic database takeover tools such as SQLMap, which automates every step in the process of a SQL injection.

Let us see it in action.

2.6.1 Hack Steps

1. Navigate in your browser to the site and page that you want to inject (with the Burp Suite Proxy enabled).
2. Attempt some normal queries against that page (e.g., type something into the form and click submit).
3. Find that submission page in the Burp Suite sitemap and left click on it.
4. On the right-hand side, find your raw request.
5. Right-click on the request and choose "Copy To File."

6. Save it in your SQLmap directory under an easy-to-remember name.

7. Go back to your terminal and cd to your SQLmap root by typing:

   cd /home/<user>/sqlmap

8. Check out the available SQLmap options by typing:

   python sqlmap.py -hh

9. We will be using the -r option which allows us to specify our Burp Suite file to determine the injection point that we would like to try. First, we will enumerate the database tables and columns by typing:

   python sqlmap.py -r file_from_burp --tables

10. Look through the output and choose an interesting looking table that will have user information.

11. Steal that table by typing:

    python sqlmap.py -r file_from_burp -T table_to_target --dump

12. SQLMap will ask if you want to attempt password cracking automatically – choose "yes"!

2.6.2 Solution: Pwning with SQLMap

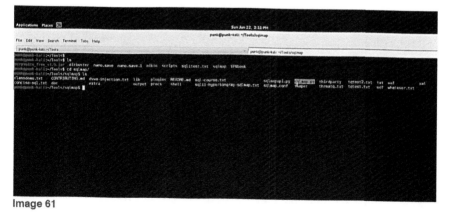

Image 61

From within my tools directory in my terminal, I want to change directories to my **SQLMap** directory. To access this I type:

python sqlmap.py -hh

Image 62

As we can see there are dozens of SQLMap options, but we are just going to be using a few of them.

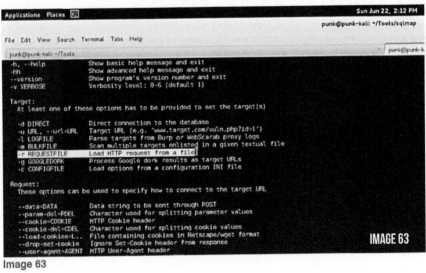

Image 63

We are going to be using the -r option that loads an HTTP request and saves time from, for example, specifying specific URLs, parameters, and so forth to test for. It is going to parse the HTTP request and use that to determine the target.

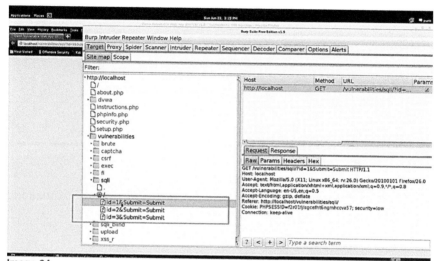

Image 64

Go back to DVWA and click around. Go into Burp Suite to make sure that "Intercept" is off but that traffic is still running through it.

Let us start by using the SQL Injection page of the DVWA normally for a bit, and then take a look at Burp Suite. To see the requests navigate to /vulnerabilities/sqli/ and check the submissions (see the box in Image 64).

Click on a request and it will populate over on the right side. From here, right-click on it and select "Copy to File." (see the box in Image 65)

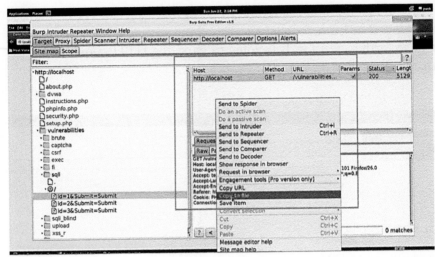

Image 65

Save it to the same directory that you have SQLMap in to make it easier. For this exercise, I will save mine as sqli-exercise.txt.

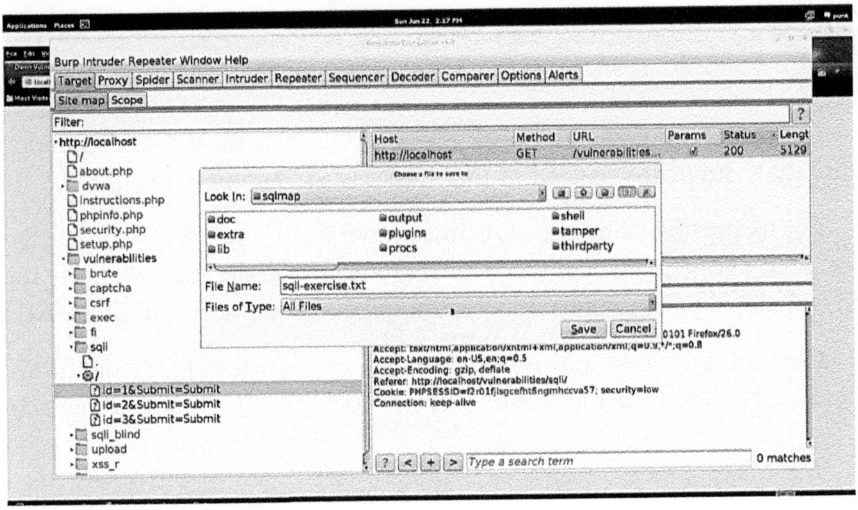

Image 66

We can make sure the file is saved by executing an "ls" command in the my SQLMap directory in the terminal. You should see your file listed there.

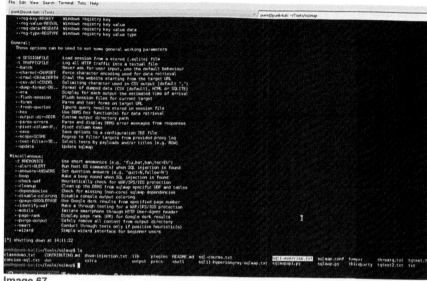

Image 67

We are going to use this .txt file to feed SQLMap. We will use this code:

python sqlmap.py -r sqli-exercise.txt --tables

We are using the --tables options to list all the tables so that we can see what is available in all of our databases.

Image 68

```
| spearphish_recipients
| type_activity
| type_actor
| type_attachment
| type_attribute_incident
| type_attribute_indicator
| type_attribute_malware
| type_attribute_recipient
| type_attribute_spearphish
| type_comment
| type_export
| type_indicator
| type_rule
| type_status
| type_user_permission
| users
| users_permissions
| whitelist
+.....................................+

Database: dvwa
[2 tables]
+.....................................+
| guestbook
| users
+.....................................+

Database: mysql
[24 tables]
+.....................................+
| user
| columns_priv
| db
| event
| func
| general_log
```

Image 69

We see here the database information schema that lists all the tables, but the one that we are interested in is the database for the DVWA – and we see that there are two tables: "guestbook" and "users."

Moving on and escalating the hack, we use that same HTTP request with additions, so:

python sqlmap.py -r sqli-exercise.txt --tables -T users -D dvwa --dump

The -T tells the tool which table we want to steal, in this case the table "users." We can also specify the database, in this case DVWA, and the --dump simply tells it to dump that database.

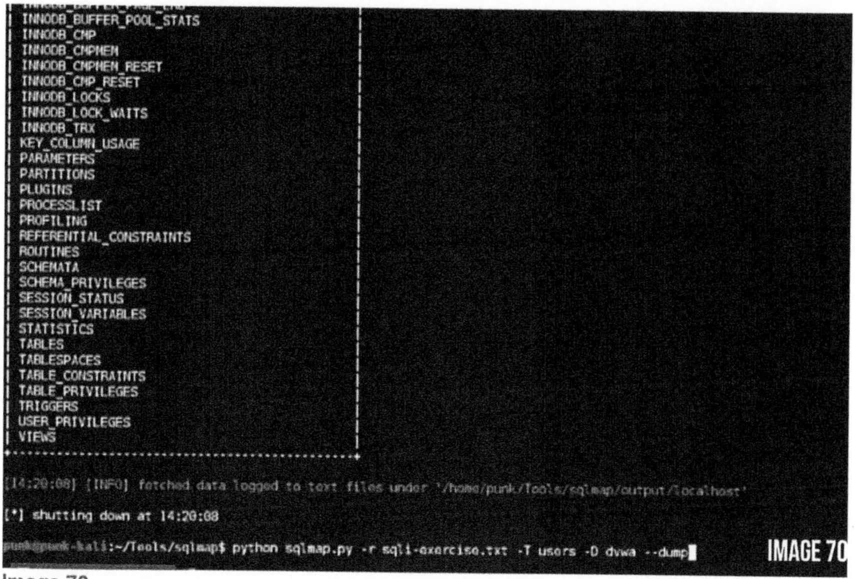

Image 70

We are prompted with a question if we would like to store hashes to temporary file for eventual further processing with other tools – the answer is yes! The next question is: Do you want to crack them via dictionary-based attack – also yes!

Image 71

In summary, SQLmap has taken the table "users" from the database DVWA and listed all of the entries. The tool has taken this data and formatted it nicely and it has also cracked the passwords!

2.7 CROSS-SITE SCRIPTING (XSS)

Cross-site scripting is another very common vulnerability.

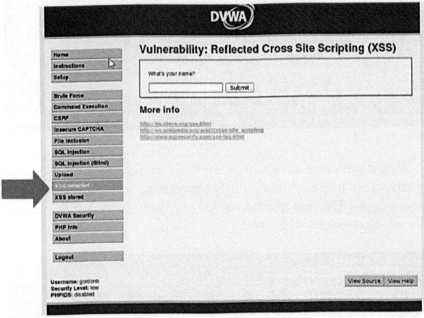

Image 72

Let us look at the XSS Reflected page in DVWA where we are asked for our name.

I am going to put "Alex" and the output prints my name. Let us see the request in Burp Suite.

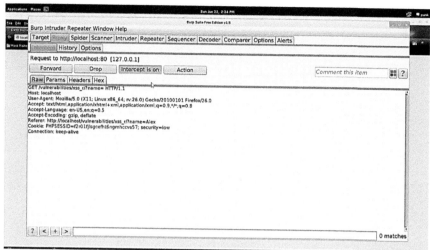

Image 73

We see that the application performed a GET request to "/vulnerabilities/ xss_r?name"

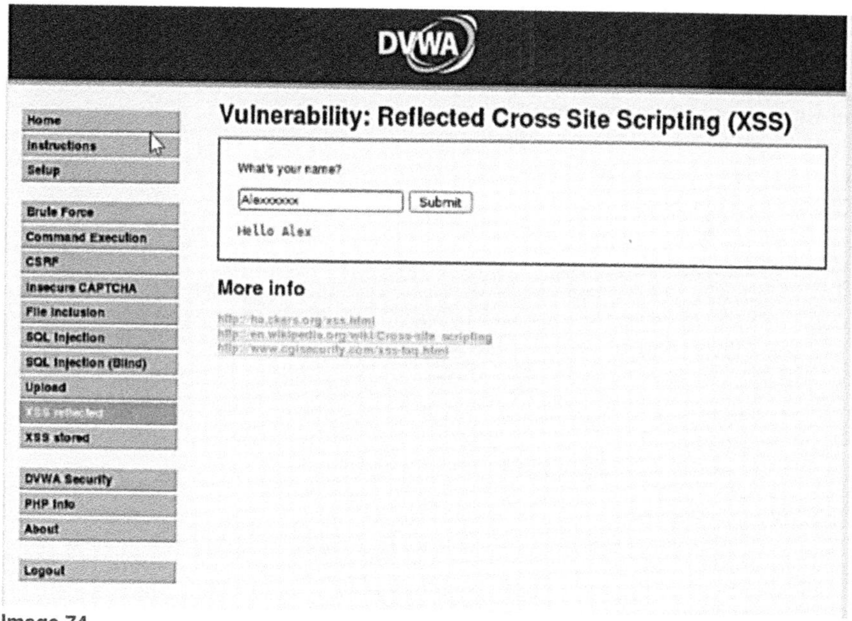

Image 74

This time let us enter my name with a bunch of x's at the end and forward this.

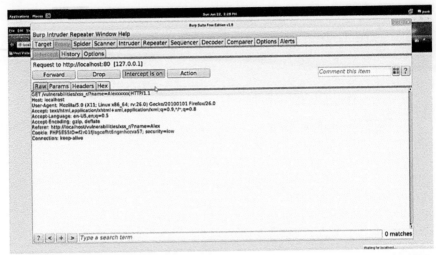

Image 75

We continue seeing that whatever is placed in the input box is being passed in to the web application through a GET parameter, in fact you can actually see the GET parameter in the URL that is being echoed back to the page.

Working with a little JavaScript we can make this dangerous, but first let us take a look at the source code for this page.

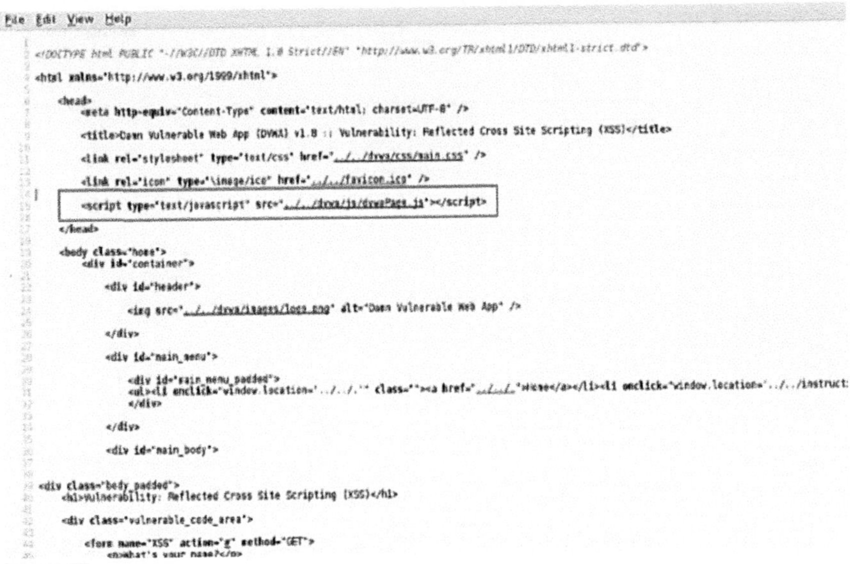

Image 76

We need to look for the script tag (see the box in Image 76) that signifies that there is JavaScript on the page (remember that JavaScript is interpreted and run by your browser).

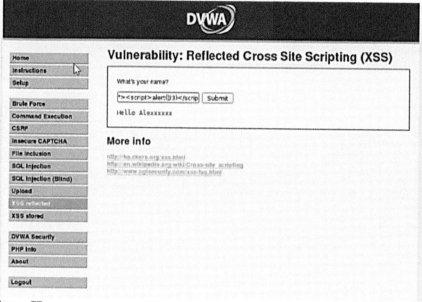

Image 77

Now let us insert a piece of JavaScript code and try to echo back an alert box that pops up and simply says "33."

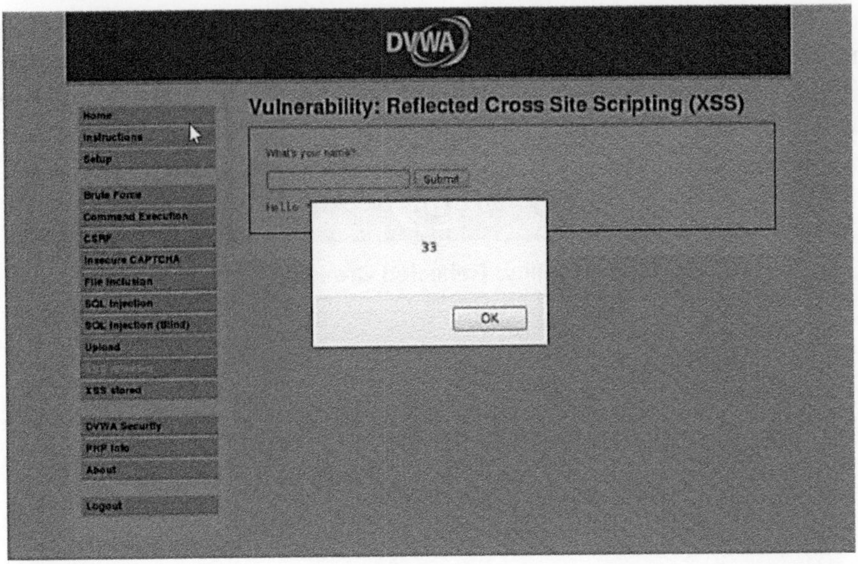

Image 78

In fact, we see that the browser executed the code, which means it executes everything in between the script tags. This means that we can insert anything we want, which could potentially be dangerous. However, are we not just exploiting ourselves by getting our own browser to execute code? The answer is yes, that is exactly what we are doing – but this same attack can be used on other people.

Attackers use cross-site scripting by crafting a link with JavaScript embedded in it, typically a GET request, and they send it to their victim. Once the victim clicks on the link, the JavaScript is executed in their browser and something bad happens. Typically this would be something like sending session information back to an attacker so that they can trick a website or web application into thinking that they are you. They can gain access to your account without stealing your username and password. Now you can see why cross-scripting is very dangerous and why you should not click on untrusted links.

2.8 STORED CROSS-SITE SCRIPTING XSS

Stored cross-site scripting is another equally bad form of cross-site scripting. This attack method allows an attacker to store JavaScript on a web app so that any time a user visits it, the JavaScript is executed.

The attack can be crafted in such a way that any user that visits a hacked page can have sensitive information stolen from them and sent back to an attacker. Having a strong password in this case would make no difference.

This type of vulnerability can also be used to deface a web page, which will be our next exercise. A quick disclaimer: *defacing a webpage that you do not own is illegal.*

2.9 SHORT EXERCISE: USING STORED XSS TO DEFACE A WEBSITE

The goal of this exercise is to deface the DVWA "XSS Stored" page with a defacement message.

Warning: This exercise is the most difficult one of this book!

Hack steps:

1. Go to "XSS Stored" in the DVWA.
2. Check out how the functionality works under normal conditions (without exploiting anything).
3. Now, try to insert your own JavaScript into the page that clears the page and replaces it with a defacement message of your own.

Hint: remember JavaScript must be enclosed in <script>enter_javascript_here</script> tags.

Hint: The "Name" and "Message" fields limit the number of characters that you can enter into the text boxes.... I wonder if there is a way around that?

Hint: You will need to use the Intercepting Proxy and the Decoder for this one.

Hint: The JavaScript code to clear a page entirely and replace it with your content is:

document.body.innerHTML="enter text here";

Make sure you get the lower case and caps straight there. Make sure when you put your text there that you include those apostrophes and the semi-colon in the string!

2.9.1 Solution – Using Stored XSS

Open up the DVWA and navigate to the XSS Stored page

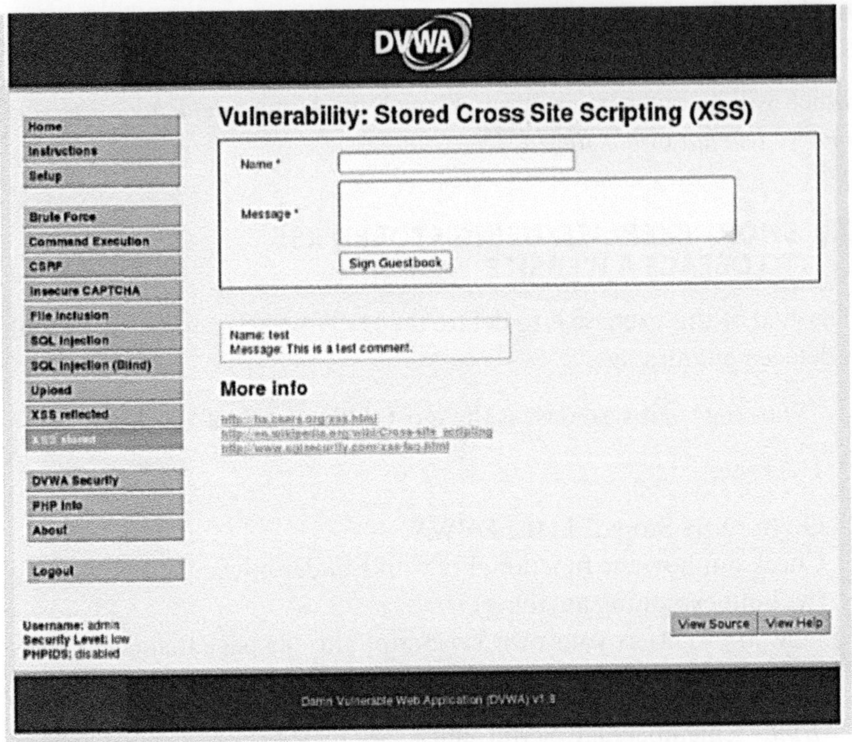

Image 79

As usual, we treat the application as an average user to understand how it all works, so let us go ahead and sign the guestbook.

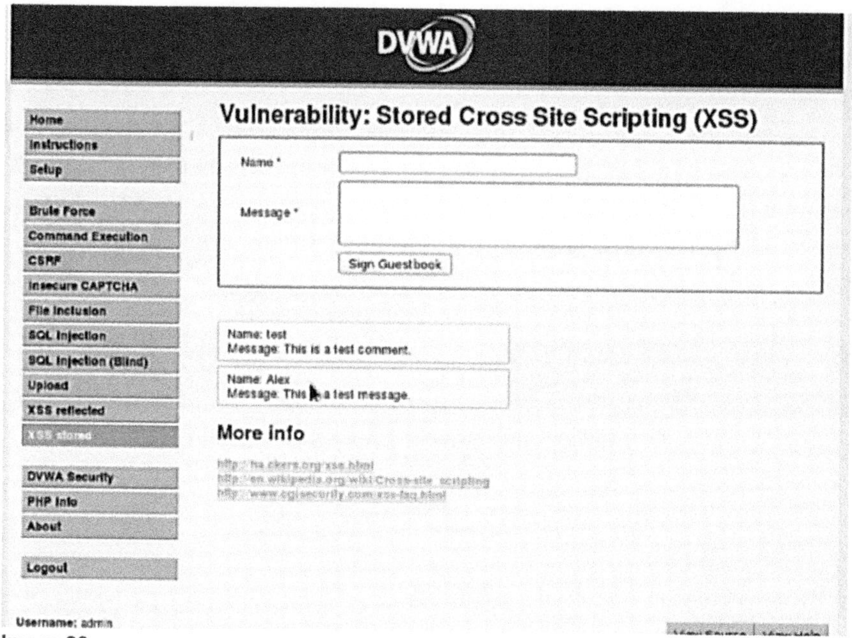

Image 80

The application is taking my name and the message that I entered and just putting that data into a box on the page. I know that the signing of the guest book is persistent because even if I refresh the page, the data stays there. Let us now turn Burp Suite "Intercept On" and see what is going on under the hood.

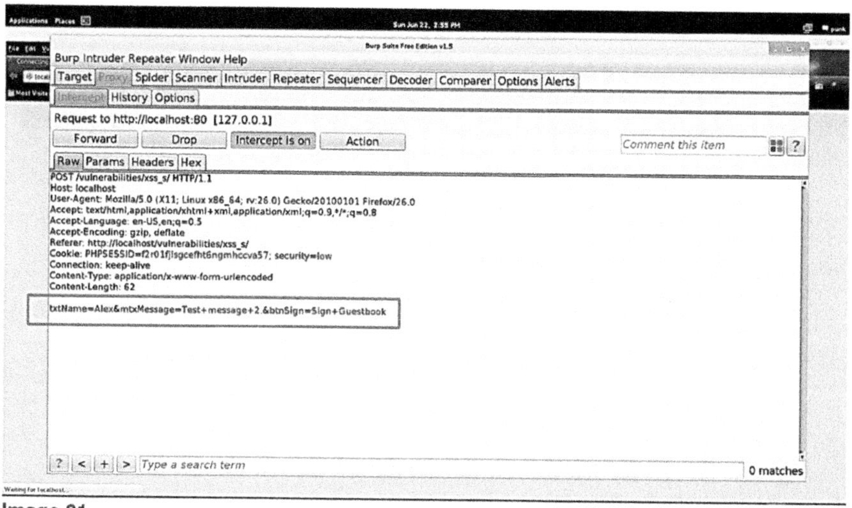

Image 81

Sign the guestbook again, intercept that request, and we can see that the application is sending a POST request to "vulnerabilities/xss_s."

A couple of other important things to note:

First, you can see that the name and message are being passed in a parameter called "txtName" "mtxMessage," respectively (see the box in Image 93). Let us now forward that along to understand the flow of the page.

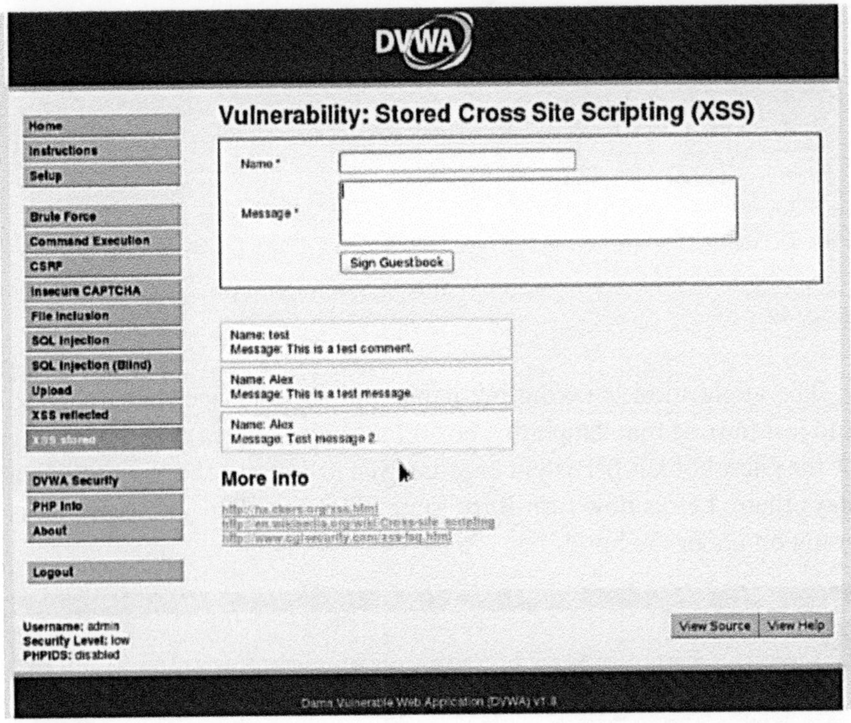

Image 82

We notice that my name and message are stored in a database and then echoed back to the page.

In order to deface this page, let us see if we can use the POST request parameters to inject some JavaScript.

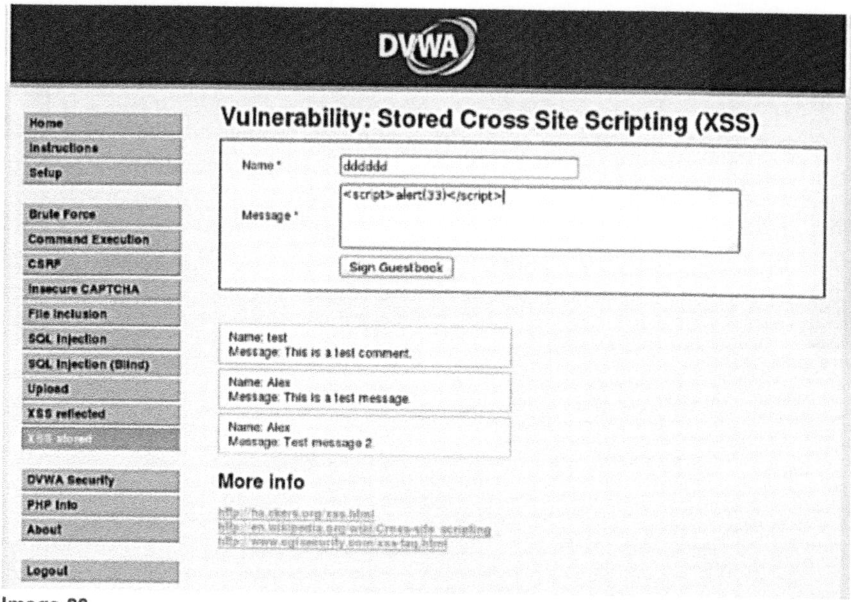

Image 83

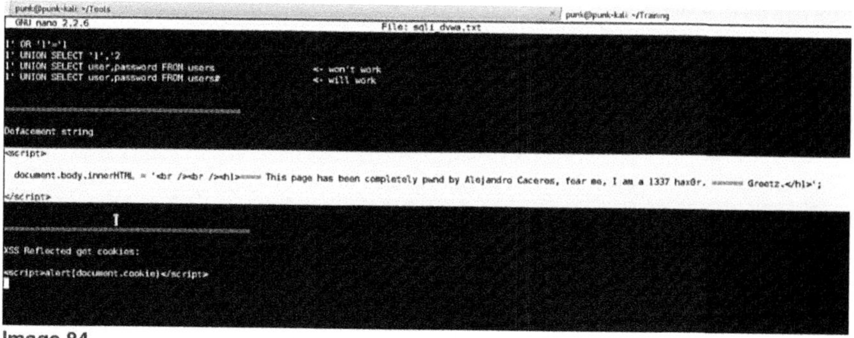

Image 84

Write your defacement message, preferably something really hacker-y, in a JavaScript string between <script> tags. Remember – we also need to encode our JavaScript defacement string.

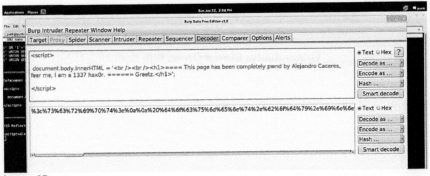

Image 85

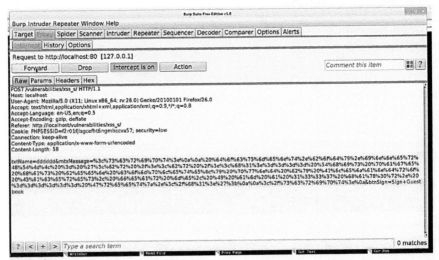

Image 86

Back in Burp Suite, we take the URL encoded information, insert it to the mtxMessage parameter, and forward that along. Let us see what happens to the application.

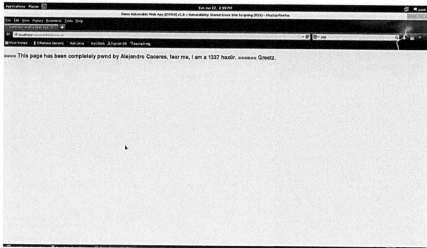

Image 87

As you can see, our XSS Stored page has been replaced by our message! Success!

As you can see, our XSS Stored page has been replaced by our image.

CHAPTER *3*

Finding Vulnerabilities

Hopefully, you have learned a little bit about exploitation in this book. The examples we have given are some of the most basic types of exploits a hacker can execute against a website. Now we will discuss how we actually find these vulnerabilities in the first place.

Hacking is all about being very mechanical and following processes as well as understanding the technologies.

Even if you are attacking a large web application, remember to always check for obvious things such as searching the pages in Burp Suite for comments. You might find a password in the developer comments – this has happened to me in a pentest before!

Ask yourself other obvious questions, for example, is the application using a content management system (CMS) like a Drupal, Wordpress, or a lesser known one? If it is, Google it! Try to find publicly available vulnerabilities and exploits. If somebody has already done the work for you, there is no reason for you to do it again. Look it up, see if there are publicly available vulnerabilities and exploits.

Next, try to discover if there is a default password on the CMS you are trying to hack. The better known ones will typically not do this, but some of the lesser known ones often will. If so, try it out on their admin page and see if the default password will work.

Look for obviously suspicious pages, for example, sometimes you can reset a user's password without actually being authenticated as that user since all you have to do is hit a page called something like "resetpassword.php."

As I mentioned, hacking a web app is a game of patience and repetition. Take notes! I mentioned at the beginning of the book that I like to have a spreadsheet open where I can make notes about things that I see, things that I find, things that I have already checked, things I have not checked.

Understand the application, understand what it is doing, how it is passing data, why it is passing data, what technologies are being used and where. After you understand the application, you should have a good idea where to find the login function for the application.

Following from this we know that the username and password are usually stored in some kind of a database and this is a great place to check for **SQL** injections. Look for other things, for example, is it echoing back a string somewhere when you enter syntax?

Always go for the obvious vulnerabilities first before trying more complex exploits.

One thing you should never ever do is run an automated scanner at an entire site because, although there are many great scanners out there, they tend to miss a lot of vulnerabilities. You need to understand the application and understand what it is doing before you can actually break it.

3.1 THE BASIC PROCESS – STEPS

First, map the entire application; discover hidden content with the Burp Suite Spider and apply some educated guessing in order to find pages to attack. Look at HTTP requests and responses when you navigate the application. Try to understand how requests and responses are being passed back and forth.

Try to understand the technologies behind the application. Is it using PHP, is there some kind of database, is it JavaScript heavy?

Following from checking the obvious, we should look towards exploiting client-side controls that attempt to stop a user from doing something through parameters in GET or POST requests. Look for attempts at stopping the user from typing certain characters into text boxes since these are often good injection points.

If somebody is stopping you from doing something on a web application there is probably a reason for it, and if you can bypass that and find the reason for them to try to stop you from doing that, it is usually a great way in.

A general note on injection attacks: always URL encode when putting characters into parameters since it never hurts but always helps.

Check for SQL injections within the applications by trying special/reserved SQL characters, for example the apostrophe symbol, pound sign, dash, plus, parentheses, and so forth.

There is a huge amount of information out there on how to find and exploit SQL injections and we have only scratched the surface.

Check for cross-site scripting by entering the string we used in generating an alert box. Look at what happens when you try this (make sure it is URL encoded), and observe the response in a browser. If you see an alert pop up you just found cross-site scripting. You could actually go out there on a lot of websites and find cross-site scripting by doing that, although you should of course never try to pentest a site without permission.

If you do not see an alert pop up, that does not necessarily mean that it is not vulnerable to cross-site scripting. You can check the responses either in Burp Suite or by simply right clicking in your browser and viewing the source. Something to check for: are your script tags being filtered or changed in some way? If they are being filtered or changed in some way, can you think of a way to bypass that filter?

There are a lot of sloppy filters out there: check out what it is doing and see if you can bypass it. Understand what the application is doing to your attempted payload and then try to shape it around that. Failing that, there are also some really good resources online for "filtering bypasses" that are very simple to use. You can pretty much copy and paste strings into parameters and often they will work, but try to understand what you are doing rather than just copying and pasting.

Be very patient and eventually you will begin to understand where vulnerabilities are most likely to occur and that will end up saving you a lot of time.

3.2 EXERCISE – FINDING VULNERABILITIES

The final stage is to Capture the Flag!

Go to course.hyperiongray.com/vuln1, follow the instructions, and use what you learned to guide you.

If you solve the challenges and capture the flag, send me an email (acaceres@hyperiongray.com) and I will give you a shoutout on my personal Twitter account and the Hyperion Gray Twitter account.

Happy hacking! I really hope that you have enjoyed this book as much as I enjoyed making it.

Printed and bound by CPI Group (UK) Ltd, Croydon, CR0 4YY

08/06/2025

01896868-0002